Under the Sign of the Lily

The Messianic Sophianic Age

The Soul on Its Path
to Perfection

The Soul
on Its Path
to Perfection

The Eternal Word,
The One God, the Free Spirit,
Speaks through Gabriele,
As through All the Prophets of God –
Abraham, Moses, Isaiah, Job, Elijah,
Jesus of Nazareth, the Christ of God

Gabriele
Publishing House
The Universal Spirit
Is the Teaching of the Love for God and Neighbor
Toward Man, Animals and Nature

The Soul on Its Path to Perfection
Third Edition, December 2019
Published by:
© Gabriele Verlag Das Wort GmbH
Max-Braun.Str. 2, 97828 Marktheidenfeld, Germany
www. gabriele-verlag.com
www.gabriele-publishing-house.com

Translated from the original German title:
Die Seele auf ihrem Weg zur Vollendung
Order No. S 209en

The German edition is the work of reference for all
questions regarding the meaning of the contents

Printed by: KlarDruck GmbH, Martkeidenfeld, Germany

ISBN: 978-3-89201-952-7

Table of Contents:

In Accompaniment

In February 1979, Christ, the Son of God and Co-Regent of the heavens, gave a comprehensive revelation about "The Soul on Its Path to Perfection," through Gabriele, the prophetess and emissary of God. At that time, it was published as a brochure. The foreword was given in revelation by the law-angel before God's throne, the Cherub of divine Wisdom, Brother Emanuel.

We may entrust you with this work, which until today has lost none of its relevance in a new edition. We would like to give you a suggestion to take with you on your way:

Over 40 years ago, many things were often spoken differently than today. For this reason, the eternal truth was garbed back then in human words that the people could then understand. Today, much would be expressed and passed on using other words.

But the truth is always the truth, regardless of how it is expressed in human words. For this reason we advise our readers not to look at the shell of the word, but to grasp the content, for it is the content that further guides the human being on the path of life and the soul on its path to perfection.

Gabriele-Verlag Das Wort

Foreword
to the Basic Levels of the Soul

given in revelation by Brother Emanuel,
the Cherub of divine Wisdom,
through the prophetess and emissary of God,
Gabriele

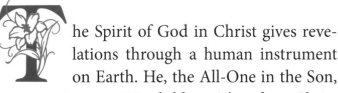he Spirit of God in Christ gives reve-
lations through a human instrument
on Earth. He, the All-One in the Son,
wants to instruct His children. Therefore, Christ
is the revealing Spirit of the New Covenant, who
speaks through this instrument in the "I Am
the light of the world." Among other things, He
teaches about the consciousness levels of the
souls, and their way home from the Earth to the
Father's house. These learning levels are transi-
tional levels or purification planes for the souls.

Before the Spirit of the Son begins to teach, an
angel of the Lord will briefly reveal the makeup of
creation.

Just as creation, every single soul, in which the eternally pure Spirit is active, is made up, created and maintained by the eternal Creator, who is our eternal Father.

His Father-Mother-Principle manifested itself from the quintessence of His creation. The heart of the cosmos is the first-created primordial work, a Primordial Central Sun. It determines the gravitational relationship to all planes and solar systems.

The primordial power, a rotating structure of spiritual magnitude, which the human mind cannot grasp in its proportions, vivifies seven further divine suns. These are the power-currents of His characteristics. Infinite planes that have, in turn, their subspheres, are connected to these seven suns. In the name of the Most Holy One, the seven planes of God are ruled by seven regents. These seven "luminaires" are called: Order, Will, Wisdom, Earnestness, Patience, Love and Mercy.

Each characteristic level cannot exist without the other six. The first creation level of God is the dominating Order, which likewise has its sublevels. They are Will, Wisdom, Earnestness, Patience, Love and Mercy. In the divine law of Order all others are also contained. Each characteristic is a heaven with sub-levels. They are further spiritual spheres, thus, seven tremendous heavens of light, which line up as a whole in the cosmic rhythm. These spiritual planes move around the Primordial Central Sun in elliptical orbits. The Earth's small solar system shows us the relationship to the primordial cosmos, its movement and its spiritual makeup.

As in a system of perpetual motion, the primordially powerful sun gives, and takes again. Through the spiritual law of gravitation of the masses, no cosmic energy is lost. Each mass attracts the other; this is how the fine-material planets are kept in place, orbiting in the great planes according to the law of gravitation. At the same time, these planes, with their unimaginably many solar systems, move in their elliptical orbits around the Primordial Central Sun. This force field is the zenith of creation.

The souls, which form the spiritual body, are made up in a similar way. In and around this spiritual garment is the Spirit, the breath of life. Thus, every spirit being possesses an ether-body, which is sustained by the odic power (Spirit). By way of personification by the All-Father-Spirit, these spirit bodies became beings that are identical with the universe. Their bodies are bodies that were created from the great whole. With this, each being is a body in the body of the All-creation. The soul also has the spiritual law of gravitation, because like all of the pure creation, it is made up in the spiritual particle structure and has the divine elements of fire, water, earth and air. Its spiritual gravitation fields are in proportion to all of creation.

Thus, this ether-body also has an inherent process of expansion, just like all divine planes can expand through the spiritual odic power, since the worlds of the eternal homeland, as well as all ether-bodies (souls) are of a fine-material nature. The love is what dominates. Every function of cosmic life expresses the divine love. It is sustaining, unifying, and, in itself, in turn, liberating, if one opens up in it, because everything is love, created by the eternal Spirit of love and eternally borne in the "now," which knows no past or future.

Thus breathes the creation of God, as does each spiritual body, as well as the spirit being, which is a body from this All-Father-Body. Each human being has this ether-body, which I would like to briefly explain.

The ether-body is the soul, which is built in the particle structure. The spiritual ether is the eternally pure Spirit, the sustainer of life. We associate the soul, which in the homeland becomes a pure ether-body, with the human being. The expression "soul" was coined by the "Fall," since through self-will, it had to successively leave the paradisiacal homeland, and went into the depths because of its own guilt. If the breath of life is violated, a different radiation tendency comes into effect, the odic power diminishes, which means that through self-will, the being of light assumes another radiation garment. Through the Fall of the spirit beings, the spiritual power was reduced and the particle structure contracted. Since the once pure spirit being became impure, the pure spiritual planes folded. To receive more spiritual power, they drew nearer to the heart of the Spirit, because the central point in each soul is the sustainer of life, the Spirit. The ether-body became smaller and the condensation increased through self-will, because the spirit beings had to leave the kingdom of purity.

Over billions of years, the human being developed, a condensed substance adapted to this material vibration. The soul folded into itself. In this way, the pure spiritual planes cannot be burdened. Thus, the soul's conscious state is near the pituitary gland and is linked with the human brain. The burdened vibration is the condensation of the physical body. Therefore, the human being as well as nature is spiritually condensed substance. The organs of life formed over the course of billions of years, because the human being has to assimilate food that is in accordance with his vibration. The pure spirit beings also partake of spiritual nourishment; it is created for the vibrational tendencies of the pure spiritual worlds. The human being's ether-body, called soul, is connected with the brain currents. Through this, the soul has become the registry of the human life. By way of the cosmic law of radiation, which is in every kinetic soul, it perceives all the details of the human life. The particle structure of the soul changes color according to our life. Whether positive or negative, everything is registered by the soul. Through its path into the depths, the soul created planes for itself, which, through Jesus, the Christ, became purification planes for it.

The radiation effects of the human aura indicate the picture of the more or less burdened soul. When the spiritual substance leaves the earthly mass, the human being, it takes this cosmic radiation with it. Through the journey into the depths, new life forms developed, whereupon the spiritual particle structure changed. They have to be dissolved through the knowledge of the divine life, so that the pure spiritual heavens can unfold. Just as the ether-body becomes smaller, so does it expand again through the extent of recognition of the life in Jesus, the Christ.

Amen.

The Soul on Its Path
to Perfection
given in revelation by Christ, the Son of God
and Co-Regent of the Kingdom of God,
through the prophetess and emissary of God,
Gabriele

First Level of the Soul
(Order)

Am the freedom, thus speaks Christ, the Son of God, through My instrument at this time. May the one who has ears, hear. The one who opens his senses will recognize Me, the Son of God, in his heart. I Am come into the world to bear witness to the life that makes the soul free. In this hour, I emphasize: that makes the soul free.

Again and again, the human being binds himself to traditions and forms and joins organizations. My life as Jesus of Nazareth was filled by the eternal holy Spirit, through which I was free.

I tried to instruct those in the temple and to win them over to freedom. They, however, wanted to teach Me, the Son of God.

I loved and love freedom. As Jesus, I recognized the eternally ruling hand of God, which can be seen everywhere.

I say to you: You are free children. My Spirit is in you. You need no traditions and do not have to belong to an organization. In you is the life. I Am this life!

If you hold a dialogue with Me every day and come to Me during the evening hours, saying: "Christ, You Savior of my soul, You are in me. I'm taking stock, debit or credit, what was positive or negative on this day, what can I do better?"– then I will dine with you at the table of the Lord every evening. The supper with the Lord is in your souls through the power of the eternal Spirit, who is active in you. Let Him work and become a flame in you, so that you recognize what a precious pearl the Father has given you – it is the power of Christ.

My dear children, thus I speak in the name of the Father, for I have assumed the mission of leading you to the eternal kingdom. The human being is unknowing. Why? Because he is rooted in traditions and forms. Become free and hear the age-old word, the divine revelation. From the primordial beginning, the Spirit of life speaks into the souls, but the human being banished the word of the All-Highest. He resorted to organizations and no longer accepted the divine Spirit, the prophetic word through a human being.

At all times, God has taught His children. Now, a new age has dawned once more, which also comes to an end for humankind. However, it brings a spiritual turning point, for the Spirit has said: "*Let there be a new Earth and a new heaven.*"

I teach for the present time, and in this hour, the first basic level of the soul – it is Order.

There are seven levels in the basic level of Order. Besides Order, they are: Will, Wisdom, Earnestness, Patience, Love and Mercy. They form the seven supporting characteristics of the cosmos. From these divine levels, seven manifested angel-princes go forth, who rule these planes and therefore, the seven basic levels in every soul, as well.

Seven basic levels, and in them, in turn, the sub-levels, all of which have to be activated by the soul, because no characteristic can exist without the other. Your spiritual soul structure is built and aligned according to the divine creation, which means that it vibrates as the universe vibrates. Your soul should also vibrate in this rhythm. The divine vibration has to be activated by every soul, and only then, can the soul return to the Father's house.

God's law is radiation. Just as this Earth is permeated by its magnetic fields, so are all the planets. No matter what the vibration and mass – everything vibrates, radiates and pulsates. All divine life is based on radiation. It permeates all systems and all heavens. It is also the life of the spirit beings. The ether-bodies, among others, are vivified by the radiation. The whole of the All-creation is in every soul, since the soul is a micro-cosm in the macrocosm. Each soul has to change and align itself with the Most High, namely, with God, our eternal Father. In the Spirit of the Eternal, the Son of God is the light of the world, who prepares every soul structure for the perfection that was given to each being by God, our eternal Father. The perfection is the life from God. In it, the divine love should be actualized.

My dear children, the level of Order is a basic level with six other sub-levels. It affiliates with this solar system. The solar system is enveloped in a plasma. No base vibration can penetrate this plasma. Everything negative, as well as the positive, falls back to the Earth and its children. When a soul leaves its earthly garment, the relatives wonder: Where does the soul go? The person should frequently ask himself this question and similar ones, not only in the case of death. Very often he could answer this question himself, if he asks the right question, for instance: How did the person live? Did he love order in his life? Did he believe? Did he recognize Christ in himself? Did he know about the eternal life? Did he know that Christ guides the soul? Did the person live the Ten

Commandments or was he a superficial person? If the latter was the case, then the soul will remain bound in one of these sub-levels of Order.

The planet Earth belongs to the sphere of the level of Order. On it, is the showplace of those bound to the Earth. All unknowing souls ask about where they will go or what happened or will happen to them. They were, among others, disbelieving people, they were murderers, gamblers, drinkers. They were once human beings who thought that their life would end with the life on Earth. Such and similar souls are on the level of Order. How do these souls that are tied to the Earth live? They live in a variety of ways, very often also among human beings! They continue to frequent their dens of vice; they fight and argue; they try to murder. If the person was a murderer, the soul remains shackled to this drive, until it accepts the divine teachings.

The unknowing, bound souls on the level of Order try to live with their own kind. This means that they cling to people, because they know little about the condition of their souls. It could be said that they live in their own world of illusion, because they did not keep the divine laws while in the earthly garment. They persist in nightclubs, celebrating and roughhousing, just as they did as human beings. When they then awaken from their delusion and are not heard by the human beings, they become aggressive and try to influence people. With this, they prove to themselves that they are alive and equal to human beings. They then feel stronger and also more knowing than the person. They also hear what is being spoken all over the world, because on their vibration level they can perceive more than human beings can. Through this, things reach people's ears that are merely partial truths or also pranks by the souls bound to the Earth. This makes the base souls feel important. This is very especially the case when a mediumistic person opens his channel to this level of vibration. The Spirit also calls this vulgar spiritism, which is not approved by the divine principle. The souls that reveal themselves through such channels have little strength for these radiations – it is taken from the mediumistic person and from the listeners. The Spirit of God does not work to increase the energy here, because He does not condone such practices.

Strive for the highest and ask your Father in Jesus, the Christ, and then ask for the servants of purity, because each child is a creature of the All-Highest. The one who surrounds himself with what is base will attract the base! The one who, in humility and love, asks for the highest and lives the love for neighbor will also attract the light, because like attracts like.

If the soul has awakened in the divine, then it recognizes that Christ is the way to become free. Through this, the soul, if it lives accordingly, can be guided further – depending on the increase of its light intensity – into a sublevel of the planets of Will, then on to Wisdom and to Earnestness, as well as to Patience, Love and Mercy. All these planets are still in the sun plasma. They form the first basic level that each soul has to work through.

My dear children, the soul can reach higher levels and spiritual planets only when it has knowledge and also lives it. The knowledge is of no use to the people and the souls if it is not lived, because each soul has to align its spiritual magnetic currents to those planets that it has opened in its spiritual particle structure.

Just as the human being belongs to this Earth and is attracted by it, so will the soul be attracted by that planet which spiritual frequency it has. Immediately after it has left its body, the soul hears tones, a kind of music of the spheres. It recognizes colors and forms. These are the vibrations of the planet and the light intensities to which the soul tends. As soon as it has unfolded, it will be attracted by them.

On the planets are spiritual dwellings that were created from the substances of the planets by the responsible spirit beings. Each planet is supervised by a spirit being. The world of the animals, plants and minerals that live there is also entrusted to him. Each spirit being guides the works of the Lord in absolute love and harmony. The souls are also instructed in this rhythm of life. If the absolute principles of Order are not accepted, the soul will remain on this planet for a longer period of time, until it accepts the teachings and also lives them. Each soul is individually guided and instructed according to its inner condition and degree of maturity.

My dear children, these learning hours for the souls are not earthly hours, instead, it can take eons of time until a soul recognizes itself. It also depends on the soul's willingness to learn. It is just like the life on this Earth. The souls are instructed just as human children are. If a human being or a soul says: "I only listened to it," then the soul or the human being remains bound. Advancement can be made only when what was heard is lived. The eternal love knows no time. It can wait patiently, until the soul has attained a degree of love. Only then, can the teaching angel proceed further. According to this goal of life, the magnet of the soul aligns itself with a next higher level of consciousness. The soul will then again perceive higher melodies of vibration, by which it will be attracted, only once it has attained a further degree of life in its divine particle structure.

The evolution of consciousness takes place according to your degree of life and love. Many souls feel quite at home on the sublevels of the basic level of Order. Some think they have already reached the kingdom of heaven, until the veil of delusion is taken from them to reveal their true condition. Only then, do they recognize their own disastrous circumstances and those of the ones who live without love and balance in their dream pictures.

"Recognize yourself" is the motto, especially on the basic level of Order. Much is taught to my soul children. Until they awaken, in human terms, it can take thousands of years, particularly on the level of Order. And it is precisely my soul-children who live on this level that strive especially for yet another incarnation, because they lack the connection of love with God and His life. The teaching angels try hard to teach and show the souls the omnipotence of God. Especially via the level of Order, the part-rays of the minerals, the part-particles or groups of souls or part-souls of the plants and animals move up. Few of these souls bound to the Earth, develop an active participation in this upward striving of the creation of life. Particularly on this level, how wonderful it is to see the evolution of the elements of creation, for they, too, are attracted by the purely spiritual planes or by high forms of life according to a certain rhythm of life on Earth. On this level, the soul lacks interest in the divine love and its teachings. Just as humankind orients its striving toward matter, so does the soul in these soul-spheres. The human saying states: "As the tree falls, so does it lie," meaning that the soul remains in the same condition as the human being lived.

The animal kingdom, which also stays on the basic level of Order, is wonderfully oriented by the responsible spirit beings. The interested souls experience how the lion lies by the lamb, how cat and mouse keep each other company, as well as cat and dog. The birds live in harmony with the crawling animals. There is no more eating and being eaten! Even for My soul-children on the level of Order, it would be a glorious furtherance to see this, if they could open their heart for it.

O see, this is how the guiding and teaching angels work. You will ask: "Where do the responsible spirit beings and teaching angels come from?"

They come from the realms of the homeland. The teaching angels as well as the guiding angels come from their own heavenly spheres. If, for instance, a teaching angel is needed on the basic level of Order or of Will, then a spirit being from the pure spiritual heavens, either from the heavenly level of Order or of Will, goes to the teaching levels. In the purification planes, or teaching planes, as they are called, the spirit beings represent the regency of the heavenly level to which they belong. They also instruct the souls according to their knowledge. If the teachings are not accepted, then, in the course of a certain spiritual cycle, the protection of the soul (protection of Christ) recedes, causing their deeds to be produced as pictures. This is meant to stimulate the soul to feel soul-remorse. When the protection of the soul recedes, the cosmic rays penetrate the soul particles. They facilitate the stimulus toward recognizing guilt. Only the Earth has a corresponding atmosphere that has a filtering effect on the radiation. Broadly speaking, this is no longer the case with all the other finer-material planets, because they have other climatic conditions. Furthermore, the soul should be stimulated toward self-recognition and toward forgiveness, as well as toward the love of neighbor!

Human heart-thinking has atrophied. They may talk about their Redeemer, but their hearts are far from the sole consistent power. Through Redemption, I have opened every level that I explain, not only in infinity, but also in each soul. The human being could be far advanced in the Spirit, because nearly 2,000 years of grace have passed. During this time, human beings and souls could have worked through several of these levels. All are granted the strength to conquer all the levels while in the earthly garment. But since the victorious Christ is not recognized, I ask: With which power do you want to be victorious? With self-love and selfishness, with the illusion of the external?

The human being himself has invented these earthly entities, and therefore, the soul is bound to them. Every soul will attain heaven, when it lets go of these earthly traits and strives for the consciousness levels of the Spirit, because it has to go through every single level.

What is an illusion? For example, your external church. When a person is rooted in church faith, the soul cannot become free, because there is no external church in the Kingdom of God. In one of the nature levels, also called characteristic levels, the soul has to free itself from its imposed spell.

If a priest is bound to the dogma, the priest's soul stays tied to the dogma. A persistently cramped soul can live in this condition for eons of time, until it recognizes the true and free foundation of Christ.

In the timeless and spaceless seven-dimensional life, there are many possibilities for expiation. That is why each soul has to be guided and instructed according to its degree of maturity.

Humankind clings to its Bibles. It talks about the quoted words of Jesus, but the fewest of My children live accordingly. When what was written is not lived, then every book, including the Bible, is useless to the people. I do not like to speak about the Bibles, because only partial truths are found in them. Through the many translations, carried out by unenlightened people, the holy work has become a human work, out of which the Spirit quotes only the remaining truths or clarifies some things. The Holy Scriptures are the papyrus rolls. They contain the high meaning of life. They are holy, because the One Holy One, My Father, inspired them.

I go back to the level of Order. The weary wandering souls on the Earth, which are tormented by narcotics, alcohol and bad words and deeds, need a lot of rest after leaving their body.

In the name of, and according to the will of the Lord, the responsible spirit being has fashioned the planets of rest that have been granted for souls in various ways. In the basic level and sublevels of Order, there are, among other things, the planets of rest. The souls are free to choose which place of rest they want. However, the planet must be in harmony with the soul's vibrations. On the planets of rest there are pine groves, restful meadows, houses, gardens. All forms and colors are for the vibration range of the level of Order. Just as the Earth brings forth its material life through the power of God, so do all the other planets. As it likes, the soul can find rest either in a garden, on a bench, in a house or on a restful meadow. However, it is constantly watched over by a teaching angel. The souls do not sleep like human beings – they rest.

The souls are granted every kind of help, but it is not always accepted. Whether the soul submits or not, whether it rests or continues to live and work among those of like mind, the irradiation will come for each soul one day, even though it may take eons. The awakener, the sun, will touch every deed someday. The light makes everything visible. Through this, each soul is led to a decision, either for further development or for a further incarnation. This is lovingly revealed to the souls by the teaching angels.

By way of soul pictures, which develop through the cosmic irradiation, they can recognize themselves and, wtih the help of a teaching angel, they can recognize the condition of their soul, but also the possibilities for their development. The teaching angel explains to them the difficulties of a further incarnation as well as the possibilities for advancement. He also talks about the dangers that a new incarnation can bring. But the cycle of eons is also indicated and the possibilities for advancement in it are explained to the soul. From the level of Order, in particular, many beings press for a new incarnation, because the former human being, as well as the soul, were and are unknowing. Not every soul accepts an instruction. The teaching angels are treated harshly by the souls, just as the person once lived and behaved.

The messengers of light are exceedingly patient, while conveying the necessary knowledge to the souls. Now and then, disciplinary vibrations of the nature, also called characteristic, of Order, have to be applied, because the perfect spirit being can draw and act from all seven characteristic vibrations. Just as the omnipresent Spirit uses his seven characteristics, which contain the four natures, and reveals Himself through the various vibration tendencies, so is it also possible for the perfect spirit beings. God, the Lord, placed the whole into the spirit body of each of His beings, but not the omnipresence. It is established solely in God-Father and in the Christ of God.

In all planes, the work of life is called: "The Homebringing of All the Children of God." What takes place in the purification planes shall also take place on the Earth. Also on the Earth, it is: The homebringing of all the children of God, through Jesus, the Christ, His Son, the Redeemer of humankind. Take note: Every picture of the future that a human being makes produces a reflection in the soul. Therefore, it is very important to live at all times in the present with God, our Father and with your Redeemer.

Anyone who leads others astray through word or deed has to expiate the burden of the temptation, until his deed has been forgiven him. Only then, can God forgive him. The one who teaches falsely must likewise expiate this. The one led astray must forgive the tempter! A soul will remain bound until the one led astray has forgiven through spiritual insights.

Therefore, heed your thoughts, words and deeds. How quickly they can become disastrous for the soul. The one who mentions a cause again and again has not yet forgiven it, even though he thinks he has. By mentioning the cause, it is called up again and again, since everything is vibration.

The one who loves My Father's creation also loves His creatures, the human beings and all higher and lower life. Endeavor to meet all the life of creation with love. Avoid the negative influences. Try to think positively. Then, My dear children, the Creator-power will awaken in the soul. It liberates your soul from the level of Order, since you have already gone through it as human beings, through the power of positive thinking.

The first basic level, the Order, also contains its sublevels. For your better understanding, I repeat them: Order is the basic level; the sublevels are Will, Wisdom, Earnestness, Patience, Love and Mercy.

I Am the life in every soul and in every human being – come to this conscious life. The one who lives in Me becomes free, as free as I was in Jesus of Nazareth. I Am the living Christ, who dwells in each soul. The Christ was in Jesus. Through the Redeemer-deed, I Am in you. The one who strives for the light of the truth in thought, word and deed lives in My Father's eternal power of blessing.

Amen.

Second Level of the Soul
(Will)

I Am the life! You should always keep these words in mind, for in accordance with My Spirit, the soul will reach the heaven of love, which I have reclaimed for it, because the meaning of life is love! Open your hearts and enter the inner kingdom where I dwell. Do not seek Me in the external world. I have come to proclaim to you the salvation of the inner being, the "I Am." I Am this eternal existence, which went forth from the Father to lead all back to the Father's house.

If only you could enter your inner spheres and recognize your own existence in this "I Am," then you would live in this divine presence at all times. O hear the word "life." Do you not stand in the limitation of death? But I, who assumed the flesh, I, who come again, namely, in My own, I live in your souls. Are not all of you My own? Did I not die and resurrect for all, so that you, too, may resurrect?

What about this "It is finished"? The word is flesh, the Spirit has aligned with the eternal Father's house, only your souls are still slumbering on this side of life.

The Spirit of the New Covenant, Christ, that gives revelations wants to awaken your souls and show you the way to the Father's house. It is only through Me that you will come into this freedom that you have in you. For this reason, you should recognize the life and not persist in the concept of death. Do not fear, for I Am with you all the days of your eternal life. Are these not wonderful words, thoughts of love? They should penetrate deep into your souls and accomplish what I spoke and speak again and again: I Am the eternal existence. This eternal existence is the Christ, who adopted the human beings and souls and wants to vivify them. I lead all to the Father, to God, our Lord, who is the life. This God is the sphere of activity in each soul. However, if you do not worship God, but only the world, then you will live long on this level of Order, which I have already explained to you.

Humankind lives on this level of Order. Why? Because it is the lowest vibration in the universe.

But God sent Me, His Son, to this level, so that the souls can reach the spheres of perfection via the Order. I also have to repeat several things in the basic level of Will for My earthly children, so that they better understand the correlations of the Spirit.

There are seven characteristics in the divine kingdom, in which are the four divine natures. They are Order, Will, Wisdom, Earnestness, Patience, Love and Mercy. They form the seven heavens that revolve around the Primordial Central Sun. The supreme star of the Father, as we want to call the Primordial Central Sun, carries all levels through the spiritual law of gravitation. You know that the masses attract one another, as do the primordial forms.

Gigantic weightless planets orbit their suns in the heavenly planes that were intended for them. The planes, also called heavens, are ruled by the manifested characteristics. They are, among others, the Sons of God. Recognize: I Am the first-born, who instructs you and will lead you through all these levels to the Father's house.

The first Fall-child, you call it "Lucifer" – as some of you know, since I taught it, is a female angel. She wanted to be like God; she wanted a divided creation! Through My Mercy, which I proffered to the world while in the flesh, I was victorious over the female angel. Creation cannot be divided, because the masses support one another. However, parts of spiritual planets were carried out of the eternal homeland into the universe. Through the negative thoughts, the part-planets condensed. Thus, your Earth, as well, is merely a part-planet, which, however, bears within all seven divine rays. The basic substance belongs to the primordial planets in the eternal homeland, which are fine-material, just as your eternal body. You, too, each and every one of you, are a body from the great All-Father body. When the spirit being goes into the depths, then the flexible soul folds into itself, which forms the body of the spirit.

A parable for your better understanding: Many flowers on Earth open only when they are irradiated by sunlight. If the sun is covered by clouds, then the flowers remain closed.

The light is the fuel of life. When the light diminishes through its entry into the Earth's sphere, then the light in the spiritual particle structure also changes. Because of this, the soul particles press toward the still remaining light, that is, they begin to fold into themselves so that they can live from the primordial fuel, the light. When the spiritual particle structure gets smaller, the soul awaits its newborn earthly garment. This means that with the first cry of the newborn child, the encased soul gradually enters the earthly garment. The light of the soul permeates the cells of the earthly garment and forms the person's aura. All the spiritual wealth that had receded should develop during the sojourn on Earth. All the burdened soul particles should become free through a conscious life on Earth. Through this, the soul can unfold and draw new spiritual powers, enabling it to enter higher regions after its course of development on Earth. If that doesn't take place, then it remains bound to the level of Order or to Will, which I now want to explain.

The characteristic of God, the Will, is a heavenly plane as well as a level of purification. It has, in turn, the sub-levels of Order, Wisdom, Earnestness, Patience, Love and Mercy, because no characteristic of God can exist without the others. Once all the planes in the soul are vivified in the Spirit of God, only then, can the child say: "The Father and I are one." No soul can live without the Spirit. The Spirit is God, and God is the power. Thus, the soul cannot live without the attributes and natures of God, for they are the inherent laws of life.

In the universe, the law is lived, and in the cosmic soul, as well. If this is not the case, then the soul has to develop, namely, from one characteristic level to the next.

Outside the sun plasma, the level of Will is likewise a purification plane with many solar systems, adapted to the vibrational tendencies of the souls. Those spirit bodies that have completed the basic level of Order with its sublevels sojourn there.

On the level of Will, the soul is aligned with the Will of God. There, it has to recognize and live what it bears within since the primordial beginnings, and what was either covered up or burdened through its life on Earth. On the level of Order, the souls were taught the thought of God, which signifies the sensation of light.

Verily I say to you, your thoughts as well as your words have an unimaginable power! Therefore, check your thoughts so that the soul can find its way out of this level of Order and pass on to the level of Will.

Since the soul is a body from the All-Father body, it has to heed the spiritual law of gravitation. Every soul has to live what it has heard. Through this, the soul particles are purified and aligned with the divine law of gravitation, because where the state of the soul is concerned, it is: "Like attracts like." If the soul has not lived the level of Will and has not practiced the divine Will, then it will stay bound to the level of Will until it totally lives this inherent law. Only then, will it have illuminated and expanded the soul particles to the extent that it can be attracted by the next level.

On the level of Will, as well, spiritual houses were created by a guiding angel, which cannot be compared to the dwellings on Earth. According to their vibrational power, they were created for the souls on the level of Will, as well as gardens and footpaths.

Every part-soul of an animal, every spiritual part-particle of nature, often merely one spiritual ray, which, for example, is contained in the minerals, has to be aligned with the divine law of gravitation. The spiritual animals also have the four natures of God: Order, Will, Wisdom and, Earnestness. Each tiny particle is fashioned according to the law of God and aligned with the all-encompassing life.

On the level of Will, the soul is also taught: Recognize yourself and your self-will. You have to totally discard your self-will. Only the Will of the Father endures eternally, for His Will is the "Let there be," a nature and at the same time, a characteristic.

The Will is thus a Creator-characteristic of God and at the same time, a nature, just as Order is "the thought." The soul has to recognize the "Let there be" and has to expiate its human wanting. This is why it goes from one sublevel to the next, in order to activate in itself the Father's law of Will.

The soul is instructed: You know about God's thought, now you have to activate in yourself the "Let there be," the divine Will, because according to the "Let there be," you may be creatively active. Thus, the soul, accompanied by its guardian spirit, goes into all the sublevels. According to the instruction of the teaching angel, it gradually aligns its soul particles with the divine law of Will.

Every soul has to learn, absorb, recognize and mature. The guardian angels as well as the teaching angels are there to prepare the souls. When the soul just says: "Oh yes, I heard it," then the teaching angel asks: "Did you live what you heard? If this is not the case, your spiritual particles will not open. Only the one who lives what he heard brings light into his cosmic soul. The one who does not align his spiritual magnetic field with the next higher level – by living intensely – will not be attracted by it. Only through what is lived will you open your soul, which can then move on to higher consciousness levels. For this reason," so speaks the teaching angel, "on the level of Will, live the continuance of the law, so that the basic level of Wisdom, in purity, also called heaven, can attract you. See, many came with you from the level of Order into the level of Will. Some have already advanced to the basic level of Wisdom. But because you merely say, 'yes, I hear', " thus the teaching angel instructs, "and do not live what you heard, you remain bound to this level.

Not your earthly intelligence is decisive. The more earthly intelligence the person has, the more difficult it will be for the soul on the soul levels! Only the divine Intelligence has eternal existence and should be heeded. On the Earth," thus the teaching angel continues, "you have let your soul atrophy, since you oriented yourself solely according to earthly wisdom."

Oh see, thus the Spirit of the Son also speaks to you: *"Become like the little children, for theirs' is the kingdom of heaven."* Not the earthly intelligence, but solely the divine truth endures eternally. The divine Intelligence will reveal itself as soon as you orient your thoughts to your Father, and do the Will of the Father.

Every sublevel of Will has to be completed, whether it is Wisdom or Earnestness, Patience or Love, as well as Mercy. Therefore, O soul, if you merely hear and do not abide by it, you remain bound.

The protégé is always watched over by guardian spirits. O you human beings and souls, recognize that you are never alone!

If the human being were to do the Will of the Father, then he could feel and also see the divine world. However, if the person does not understand the light of the world in the "It is finished," how can the light open the soul? Oh see, the soul then remains bound for a long time, until it recognizes the One who gave it the "It is finished." Through Love and Mercy, I, Jesus, the Christ, have opened all the levels that I explain.

Oh recognize that even in the basic level of Will there are the so-called child-souls. In reality, they are souls that disembodied while still at the age of human children. Since the soul absorbs every thought, it also reacts naively like a child.

With much patience and love, the teaching angels release the souls from their ecclesiastical ideology.

There are also children in the eternal homeland, because there are also spiritual families in the eternal homeland. I will teach you about the eternal homeland later, when you have heard about the levels of your souls. The realms of the children, that's how we want to call them, take in those souls that disembodied as children. After My "It is finished," these realms of the children were created by the power of the eternal light. Responsible spirit beings set up playgrounds and spiritual dwellings through the power of the divine thought.

Many of my explanations may sound like fairy tales, but the kingdom is alive, much more alive than the human being ever imagined! I am not telling you any fairy tales, but about the levels of your souls, which every soul has to complete.

By way of a lifeless toy, for example, a stuffed animal, the child-soul will be led to a living animal, and will thus be taught its relationship to the animal world. In the kingdom of life, the animal has no fear; only the animals on Earth do! Through the teaching angels' power of Will, the animals come to the children, who then touch them joyfully and who are then also allowed to play with them. Through this, their souls develop spiritually. In this way, the so-called child-souls are weaned from the rigid lifeless toys, like stuffed animals, dolls, etc.

The little souls of the so-called children open much more quickly for the divine power, which they accept without hesitation, than the soul that was maltreated by an adult human being. In this way, spiritual energy flows into the soul particles, by which the soul matures.

In this and similar ways, the child-souls are guided via material things to the core of life, to the Spirit in the soul. Again, the teaching angel says: "Do you want to set out on a path with a 'vehicle' (toy)?" The responsible spirit being creates a vehicle. Now, it says: "So, move it!" After a while, the child's soul feels again the inner power of life. It sets the vehicle aside, which then returns to the primordial substance, since more spiritual particles have opened in the child-soul that cause a new notion to come up. "Why a vehicle?," thus the question. "I have the power of movement in me, I feel myself lifted and go much faster than with a vehicle."

Oh see, that's how these child-souls, too, are patiently prepared. It is carefully brought home to them that they are a perfect being, which should be guided into the spiritual kingdom, into perfection. People often say: "The poor children, they had to leave their life so young!" Now you realize how prevailing is My Father's grace. Many children do not burden themselves on this side of life anymore. Therefore, they pay off their debt more quickly, and thus, often a great karma.

They go very quickly via the level of Order into the level of Will, and joyfully further on, because they learn more easily and live what they learned.

Most child-souls are no longer interested in going into an earthly garment via the level of Order, unless they are advised to do so. They have recognized what life, what the homeland, what movement, is. They feel the kinetic soul that contains everything.

Verily, I say to you, you must open all these planes, you must activate all these sub-levels. Oh begin, begin on this Earth, because each plane can be an eon for you. You can get through them quickly or less quickly, it depends on your will. The "Let there be" is the Will of the Lord.

The radiation of the Earth has not yet been taken from all the souls on the level of Will. Until the four creation-characteristics, also called natures, have been completed, the radiation of the Earth remains in the soul. We call the four creation-characteristics the spiritual stabilizers of the soul, because the soul is meant to stabilize in these four creation-characteristics, also called natures of God.

I name the four natures or creation-characteristics.

They are: Order – the thought; Will – the "Let there be"; the deed – is the divine Wisdom; the Earnestness – the Creator-love. Each soul has to make an effort to achieve these four stabilizers, in order to move on to the other three characteristics of Patience, Love and Mercy, which are before the gate to heaven. Whoever has reached the three filiation attributes is a so-called semi-angel, who teaches brothers and sisters on other levels and serves them. Although many souls know about their state, the attraction to the Earth is greater than the strength to go to the Father's house. Why? Because they see the endless vastness that they still have to work through.

Therefore, O human being, listen to the voice of your Brother and to the voice of your Father. Listen to the Redeemer, who I Am. I want to teach humankind, because the soul in the human being has years to learn and to put into practice all that the discarnate soul often cannot accomplish in an eon. Therefore, the Homebringing Mission and these lessons, for the time approaches in which the years go by, and then the soul will be in its soul-garment and in the time of eons.

The Master's call is meant for your souls:

When will you recognize the light of your true consciousness?

When will you put your thoughts in order?

When will you do the Will of the Father?

When will you recognize the deed of God, His eternal Intelligence?

When will you see the earnestness of this time?

When will you recognize the Earnestness of God, who says: "My law is irrevocable."

That is why He said: "There will be a new Earth and a new heaven." – With this, He, the great All-One, was indicating Order.

The human being can seldom understand My words, and that is why he accuses God. Again and again, the God of love sent prophets to teach humankind. However, the human being did not, and does not, believe them. Many of My children who hear Me have doubts and opinions, wondering whether it is truly I. The Pharisees and scribes also said: "The Nazarene claims to hear the voice of God. We," so they said, "are commissioned by God, because we studied His Wisdom for many years."

I said to them and also say to you: "Become like the little children, for theirs is the kingdom of heaven." If you do not become like the little children, the Spirit of life will not develop in you. Only through childlike belief and trust can you hear My voice, which reveals itself in your souls in the "I Am." I Am the eternal existence, for the Father and I, we are one! That is why I say to you, My children, I have taken on the leading back of God's children. Examine yourself, ask yourself: "Where do I stand? Am I on the level of Order? If I cannot put my thoughts in order, I cannot love my neighbor. If I hate, then I will be on the lowest level. If I cannot forgive, I will stay bound again. The one who forgives, who loves, strives higher."

O human being, recognize this, because you have found grace before God, your Father, through Me, His Son. If you bear hatred against your brother, then you hate the Father, because in every single one is the power of the eternal holy Spirit. The words "It is finished" are the Christ, who is the light of the world.

The human being should awaken and recognize himself. Every single one is free through the sacrifice on Golgotha. All souls will become free, as they recognize and walk the levels of life. Have no fear, the grace of God is with you. All these levels can be achieved through the grace of the eternal Father!

The light penetrates the world and the souls. Walk consciously toward the eternal life, for the light is the faith that opens the conscious life. Say again and again: "I am a child of God – and so are you."

Why does Satan rage in the external world? Why are people enslaved by the Satan of the senses? Because they turn away from God. They do not keep the commandments; they do not believe in the divine existence. But God, the Lord, is near you at all times. Again and again, I stress: He is the head and you are the members.

As long as the person moves, the Spirit, which fills the person with love, is in him. I prepare for you the pathways to the eternal Jerusalem. It is a struggle for the person and soul, until the soul recognizes the indwelling life and the I AM.

Your deeds are in your soul. Eradicate them. Hear the voice of the master teacher of the New Covenant. Come to Me, I go with you through the Order, to the Will, where there are already more light-filled systems, although the radiation of matter is still in you.

Enter the life! You have heard: "Verily, I say to you that the one who opens only his external ears cannot believe these words. As soon as you have opened the inner ears, the soul will have its enrichment" – that is My Will! O listen with the inner ears and live. Live the law of the Spirit. Align your thoughts with God, because through the divine thought, which is a divine sensation, you will complete all these basic levels and sub-levels on this side of life.

God, our eternal Father, sent Me to teach humankind. I will teach until the human being has said the "Amen" to this world, but the Spirit in the "Amen" says: The "Amen" is the one who carries you further, into the eternal substance of God. I Am in the Amen, My children.

Third Level of the Soul (Wisdom)

The consciousness of My Spirit is in all My children. In this hour, it is revealing itself in the word. Verily I say to you, My kingdom, as well as your kingdom, is not of this world. Nevertheless, you have chosen the Earth as your kingdom, in order to purify yourselves and again enter the light, which is the soul's patrimony.

You are people who seek the light. Where do you seek the light of the world? In the external world? Never! It is not to be found on this Earth, only in all living Being. Penetrate the depths of your true, eternal consciousness, then you will find the salvation that is the primordial light. Your true body is in your human being. The human being is the image of My Father. He walks over this Earth, so that his spiritual body, which lives in him, may become free – that is, free from guilt, and thus, also free from the incarnations that signify the guilt.

The human being knows only of his present life on Earth. The other incarnations are concealed, because the person should live in the present. Salvation is in the person. Christ, the revealing Spirit, which I Am, guides you back to the Father's house via the development levels, which we also call consciousness levels or purification planes. I, the master teacher of the New Covenant, have explained to you the level of Order as well as the level of Will. Now, I want to reveal the level of Wisdom to you. All these levels can be walked only via the power of Redemption. Redemption is the same as mercy, because without mercy it is not possible for the soul to enter the kingdom of perfection.

The kingdom of perfection is the soul's home-land. In its primordial structure, the Earth also belongs to this perfect kingdom. The soul is born from all substances, it is nourished and carried by them. The Spirit is the raw material of life. All levels that I explain are spiritual levels. They are in your souls and will open as soon as you have completed them through a positive life. The level of Wisdom is a level of creation. It is the justice and thus, the deed. God had the first thought, it was and is a sensation – it is the Order. God had the first Will, again, a sensation – it is the "Let there be." God created through His Intelligence, through which everything took place in the deed.

All spiritual levels, also called heavens, are in you. Every single soul has to actualize them through the power of Redemption. The Spirit of Love is always ready to serve the person and the soul, but the person, as well as the soul, has to come to this Spirit of Love. How often does a person seek Him in the external world? He is not to be found in forms or traditions, nor in customs either. Instead, the Spirit is free – He lives in each soul. You should be the house of the Holy Spirit. As soon as the person enters his conscious, eternal self, the Spirit will give him strength, courage, enlightenment, and show him the way to the eternal Father's house.

We have now reached the level of Wisdom with thoughts and words. The souls have put their thoughts in order and aligned themselves with the Will of God. These are teaching lessons, also called breadths of insight, which gradually open in the soul. Through this, the soul receives the corresponding light, by which the Order, as well as the Will, open – if the soul has completed both levels.

Now the soul should recognize and also live the light of Wisdom. All the planes have to undulate in the spectral lights of the cosmos. Your aura has to primarily be one single sea reflecting gold and silver. Then you are free.

Now the soul is on the level of the deed. Again, it is planets – as I have already described – which are more like the primordial substance, nearly weightless, yet still afflicted with some Earth radiation. I taught that when the soul has behind it the four stabilizers – I repeat: they are the four creation-characteristics, Order, Will, Wisdom and Earnestness – only then has the Earth radiation been taken away. The souls likewise live on planets. Why do we call them "souls" and not "spirit beings"? Because the ether body is still burdened.

Once the souls have advanced to the purification plane of Wisdom, they have already completed the levels of Order and Will.

My dear children, thus I speak on behalf of the eternal Father, for the Christ of God has taken on the leading back of all souls. Leading back means: Recognize yourself; live the divine laws. Only then, can the soul enter the eternal Father's house. The one who does not recognize the truth, who does not live what he has recognized, cannot return to the Father's house. That is why one level after the other has to be gone through. This means that the power of God, which is in you, has to be actualized.

The realms of the children are also on the planets. These souls create and recognize: "Here, for the first time, I can transform my thoughts and my will into the deed."

You have heard of the responsible spirit beings. You know about the teaching angels. At all times, the person, as well as every single soul, has at his side a spirit being. You are never alone or unobserved. Each soul bears within the power of the holy Spirit. It keeps everything in movement. In this way, the soul bears the eternal life and is, just like the pure beings that accompany it, a child of the cosmos.

How does a teaching angel instruct the soul? It says: "Rejoice, the power of Wisdom has attracted you. You have completed the level of Will. Now, you pass on into the deed. But remember: God is just. Everything that you now create has to come from the just deed, otherwise your desires will not be actualized. Your thought has to be a perfect thought in God, and your will, as well."

The dwelling places, which you call houses, will return to the primordial substance as soon as the spirit beings that have inhabited the houses are led forward. More advancing souls will come to the planets, and they, too, may create.

What does a soul desire that has passed from the lower levels to a higher one? Often, only what it could not have as a human being on the level of the Earth. It desires objects, which the Earth produces. The teaching angel says: "Now try it, take the thought, but I advise you to have thoughts about God; take the will of God and create." The soul begins to create. It takes up a thought, vivifies it in the Will and tries to manifest it in the deed – it is the divine Wisdom. But the deed did not become the manifestation that the soul imagined. Why not? Because there were still sensations of the world in what it imagined.

Now the teaching angel becomes active: "It was said that you should avoid the world. What you desired exists only on the Earth. This raw material of the Earth will pass away, because it is not like the primordial material. The divine gifts come only from that planet that bears your vibration. Therefore, you can create only what is spiritual and accessible to your momentary vibration."

Every single soul is also individually taught on the level of Wisdom, according to its soul burdens. The souls may create or fashion their dwelling places, that is, actualize them in the deed. The joy of being able to do something is great, because on the level of Order, as well as on the level of Will, there was only learning, recognizing and living. But now it is, recognize and actualize in the deed.

Oh see, all these divine gifts of development are in you – they only have to be awakened. When I say they have to be awakened, then I want to say to you: Your ether body is immortal. Even if it takes eons of time, you have to complete all of these levels, because they are in your soul. These spiritual levels are the makeup of your spiritual body, which perfects itself through development. Thus, each soul has to activate all levels, also the sublevels in the basic levels, otherwise, it will not come into the next higher level of development. The spiritual law says: The soul progresses only through attraction, however, only by first aligning its soul particles with the gravitation field through the thought – that is, sensation – through the will and through the deed.

Thus, on the level of Wisdom the soul goes from one sublevel to the next, to attain what was given to it by the Spirit of God as its patrimony. This sounds like a tale, but it is the makeup of your spiritual body that has to perfect itself again. You say, "When my heart doesn't function well, then my life is hard. When my stomach doesn't work well, then I have discomforts. When lungs and spleen are not in order, etc., then I don't feel well." – The human being goes over his Earth with many ailments.

Oh see, in the homeland there are no ailments at all. Only your soul burdens bring them out. They are the illnesses of this world. What the soul absorbs from the world into its spiritual structure, has to be reduced by it again. Thus, it needs to become spiritually healthy. This is possible for it through the Redeemer-deed of Christ. The soul is given spiritual strength from one level to the next, if it asks for this by showing its willingness and actively working for it.

As a soul on the level of Wisdom, you can also hear and not put into action, but then you will remain on this level until you have recognized that you should put into practice and also live what you have heard. Only then, will your soul cleanse itself. Through this, you can strive further toward the All-One Spirit of Love. Love – a word of this world. But the one who does not have love for his neighbor will remain a sounding gong and a clanging cymbal for so long, until the bells of the soul ring in the sound of love. Do not think that these levels are not to be reached. They are to be reached – but only through the power of God. And they are only reached once the soul and the person live according to His commandments. The love for one's neighbor is the willingness to help and to have mercy, good thoughts and a charitable heart.

With My words, I return to the level of Wisdom.

The intelligence of God is the Wisdom. God created all Being. Through this, the firmament breathes according to His Will. The planets bear the Order as does every spirit being.

If the human being would only live the Order, and follow the law of God, which is this characteristic and nature, because Moses, the keeper of Order in the spirit, the bearer of the nature of Order, brought humankind the Tablets of the Law. How little the commandments are lived. This is why the soul is rooted with the Earth and why it often wears an earthly garment. With the fulfillment of the commandments, the discarnate soul could go from this Earth into higher levels. The person would be healthy, because a healthy soul also lives in a healthy body.

My dear children, in the soul that is on the level of Wisdom, the creative Spirit of God finds more and more expression, as does the divine Will, in order to strive forward and actualize everything in the deed. This is why there is the drive to teach in the basic levels of Order and of Will, what it has already absorbed in itself and gone through.

Over and over again, souls on the levels of Order and Will, as well as Wisdom, tend toward the world. They very often slide back because they want to rejoin their relatives. There is no separation through the omnipresent Spirit, who is the great unity, which means: "One for all and all for One." The souls on the basic level of the deed try to actualize this realization. They want to also help and be effective in a dynamic way on this Earth! This is why they go again and again to their relatives and give them an understanding of the salvation of life. A thin veil separates this side of life from the beyond. How, asks the human being, can I remove it? I answer: By way of faith and of trust, with the devotion to the one Spirit, for He is the helmsman of all good things.

The request to teach on the lower levels is granted to the souls on the level of Wisdom. A teaching angel accompanies them into the depths. In this case, the teaching angel is also the guardian spirit of the still maturing soul. The guardian angel completely envelops the soul in its aura. Through this, the soul is protected from the Earth's radiation, because the Earth's radiation attracts souls that have not yet fully matured.

When a soul is released from an earthly family, to which the soul on the level of Wisdom once belonged, then to the joy of the newly discarnate soul, the further developed soul may show itself. The soul on the level of Wisdom instructs the newly discarnate soul. It gives it an understanding of the first concepts of the divine law.

The soul from the level of Wisdom is not yet totally free from the radiation of the Earth. It is, itself, frequently admonished by the guardian angel, for instance: "Do not let yourself be attracted by the Earth and the discarnate soul. Enter even more into the consciousness of God and remain in it. In your thoughts, do not go to the level of the Earth anymore, and do not long for another incarnation anymore." – The soul is merely admonished. However, it can decide for itself.

When an Earth-laden soul incarnates, it has to take part in several spiritual schoolings. To each soul that goes to incarnation it is revealed what it might encounter on its path on Earth. The many doubts, which you still often have, are also in the Earth-laden soul. If it does not believe in the one path and in the truth, if this is its will, it goes to a new incarnation.

When a well-known soul-being goes to a new incarnation, often a soul on higher basic levels begins to reflect: "Why did this being that I know go to another incarnation?" It sometimes happens that the second soul leaves the protection of its guardian angel. It forgets all the good teachings and progress it made and goes to another incarnation again, to help the newly incarnated brother or sister. Thus, very many souls also go from the level of the deed to help. They often go even though they already have the power of the light. They have already completely absolved two levels and the third one is not unknown to them. Nevertheless, they incarnate via an ascendant meant for them – as you call the planets that irradiate the cosmic soul.

Verily, I say to you, also in this case, very often the Spirit is the helmsman. He leads the soul from the deed together with the soul that it knows from the level of Order. This means that two people who lived with each other in former times now live together again. They no longer know anything of what was before. That is good, because the human being lives too much in the past and in the future. I say to you again and again: Live in the present! Recognize, the soul lives in the eternal "now," and the human being should cleanse and prove himself in the "now." This is how you should think – "Now I have the chance to purify myself quickly, so that I may return to the Father's house more quickly."

My dear children, the power of the "I Am" is Mercy – It lets no soul fall by the wayside. However, if the human being does not awaken the divine Spirit that wants to be your helmsman and guide – how often do you separate yourselves from this all-encompassing power – then the person asks: "Where is God?" And God answers: "You did not call Me during your life. You were not merciful. You were not kind. You did not live in consonance with the commandments. This is why you have become Earth-laden and deaf. Thus, you have loaded even more guilt upon yourselves. All your guilt has to be expiated. You have to complete one level after the other, so that through the power of Mercy, through the 'I Am,' the soul finds its way into the realm of light. The 'I Am' is the life, which accompanies you on all levels. The 'I Am' is the eternal existence, the power of love that never passes away. Every single soul is immersed in the power of love and regenerated by it. If you do not long for the love, you will not be carried by God's love into the kingdom of perfection, because soul and person have their free will. According to its condition, every soul will remain on a purification plane until it recognizes and lives what the divine calls for."

Through His unending Love, and following His Thought and Will as well as His Wisdom, the Spirit will guide you further to a next-higher consciousness of life, to the level of Earnestness. Nevertheless, for now, I will stay with the explanations about the Wisdom.

Oh see, there are also children's realms on the level of Wisdom, which I already taught you about on the level of Will. On the basic level of the deed, the child-souls realize that childlike ways come to an end. They mature to perfect spirit beings of another dimension. Many of these souls, which are guided via the children's realms, frequently contact a parent of the world, particularly when the soul of a parent leaves its body. The tendency of a child-soul is no longer toward the world. Its path is the path to the Father's house. How often do the parents on Earth weep and long for these little ones. I say to you: Their souls mature much more quickly than the soul of an unknowing, obdurate human being, because during its time on Earth, the child-soul no longer burdened itself so much. On the contrary, through a short incarnation, such a soul expiated much guilt. The childlike soul, which is brought to maturity, recognizes the beauties of the spiritual life. It feels at home on every level.

Recognize the power of the Christ. Jesus said: "*No one comes to the Father but through Me.*" You wonder: "What about all the dissidents who do not recognize You, O Master?" Oh see, they, too, pray to God. Even though they do not believe in the Christ, in the light of the world, the resurrection and the life is nevertheless in them.

I once said to My disciples: "Go out and spread the Gospel in all countries!" The human being is complacent in his prosperity. In the organization and in tradition he feels like an illustrious, earthly spirit. But these words are meant especially for him: "Go out and spread the Gospel in all countries." Unfortunately, this has not happened until this very day, because the person favors what is material and pleasant. Those who call themselves representatives of Christ will share in expiating the lot of those whom they did not teach, out of tradition and laziness. Through the power of God, these unknowing souls will also reach the four stabilizers, because they believe in a God and in a power that directs and guides them. As soon as these souls enter the filiation attributes of Patience, Love and Mercy, they will have to recognize and live the fundamental power of the Christ of God – only then, will the gates to perfection open.

Oh see, how important it would be to bring the true Gospel to the people. It is the power of the Christ in each individual. It is the Redemption and liberation that lead all to the Father's house. Consider the little word "all." It means that all are equal before My Father's countenance. There should be no rank and no titles, either, only servants of neighborly love. Then, the level of Order would not be overfilled with unknowing, bound souls. On the level of Order are all those who did not live the words that mean, among other things: "Carry the Gospel into all countries." Christ should be recognized in all hearts and particularly in this world, because the Earth is the school of the children! On it, you should fulfill the first commandment: "Love your God and Father above all, and your neighbor as yourself."

My dear children: do not reject the words. They should be absorbed not only by the ear, but by the heart and the soul. There, they should resound day after day as a melody of love. Make an accounting in the evening hours and ask yourselves: "Have I already developed out of the level of Order, or am I in the Will, or even in the deed?" You can check yourselves. Are you already in the deed, are you active in the Will of God, in His Order and in Earnestness? Do you recognize the earnestness of life, do you know that each child has to be saved, are you active in Patience, in Love and in Mercy? Do you realize that every single one is a brother, a sister? You say that it is difficult to live according to the commandments of the Lord in the present time. I say to you: The present time is the reflection of earlier deeds, because causes were created. The effects are the results of the causes.

The world has its laws. They should be combined with the divine commandments.

However, the disunity of the Christians does not allow this. Therefore, the question is asked again and again: "Why not the death penalty?" The Spirit says: I have given you the commandments. They are eternally valid! Mankind has sinned for thousands of years. The human being has not entered intercession, but entered the cause more and more. One day, the effect will come. So recognize the effect on the whole Earth.

Because the person is unknowing, he does not know why he has to bear this lot or fate. Bear everything with patience. Then the Father in Christ will help and support you and give you more strength. Everything has to be expiated. The Christ of God is the Helper in your need – come to Him! Take the peace, My child, that the Lord gives your soul again and again. Through His power and His blessing, the person and the soul will go over this Earth and will complete one level after the other in the known school on Earth.

You have heard: "The Spirit permeates matter." Heed these words! The more you love, pray and devote yourselves to the eternal Spirit, the more strongly the person will feel the central power of God. With this, the Spirit can permeate matter. The consciousness levels of the Spirit are linked with the nerve centers and with your organs. They alone bring forth the light that the person can develop through positive thinking. Therefore, develop yourselves in the Spirit of God. Live in love and try to work in God's energy of the deed, then you will also go through the basic level of Earnestness more quickly and be in the three fil-iation attributes, which are close to the kingdom of perfection.

My kingdom is not of this world! I came into this world as Jesus. I assumed flesh and took upon Myself the burden of the earthly existence. All the burdens that you bear as human beings, I have also borne. I was spared nothing. I know what it means to be a human being and that is why I can understand my children so well!

Through My speaking instrument, I penetrate the human hearts with the word of life, in order to enlighten the human being and the soul and to help them, in order to proclaim to you the word of life and tell you how very much Christ empathizes with you. I want to enlighten every heart, and thus guide each soul further toward the high and perfect consciousness, which is the Spirit and not matter. Please recognize the word "Spirit."

Life as a human being can be agonizing. The one who regards what is of the Earth as secondary and the eternal Spirit as primary will orient himself according to the Spirit. Through this, over the course of his years on Earth, he will feel the Spirit, which permeates the soul and matter. Live with the Spirit, and you live with your Father in heaven! Live with the Redeemer-Spirit, which I Am, and you will feel Me in you, and then the earthly agonies will lessen and the person, as well as the soul, will attain the freedom in God. The one who develops the longing for My Father, who dwells in him, will communicate with Him. You can do this every day through the power of prayer and the stillness. Love the stillness. Try to escape the noisy world for several hours so as to hold a dialogue with God, your Father. Then God will hold a dialogue with you, for the Father and I are one!

You are children of God. Before God, you are *all* equal. There is no difference. Only the world makes differences, but not the Spirit. Love one another, help and serve each other, then you will recognize that life on Earth can be borne and easily overcome. I lived and endured it. As a human being, I often felt weak and thought I could not bear this life on Earth, as well as the people with their opinions, with their self-will.

Oh see, then I went into the stillness. You can do this, too. Go into the woods; walk over the fields. God, your eternal Father, encounters you everywhere. As Jesus, I also had to learn this to find the stillness in Me.

My soul became peaceful and devoted to God, by which I fully attained the seven levels during My life on Earth. You say: "You were and are the Son of God." I repeat what I have often told you: You are all sons and daughters of the eternal Father. I have placed you on the same level. God is the Love – just as He loves Me, so does He also love you, and just as He loves you, so do I love you, I, the Liberator of your souls.

Therefore, enter the deed and actualize it through the positive thought, through the Will of God, by acting positively. Say again and again: "Lord, Your Will be done."

Soon after becoming discarnate, the one who does His Will will be able to create on the level of Wisdom, if he set out on the level of Wisdom while in the earthly garment.

The human being is on the Earth to learn and to regenerate his soul, so that the soul may find its way home to the Father's house.

The motto of every soul should be to be at home in eternity. Your eternal dwelling places are at home in the eternal kingdom. There, houses are conceived from the primordial substance, which have long been uninhabited. Possess the inner kingdom, the Kingdom of God, which, from the primordial beginning, has been prepared for you through the Father's love. You are children of this love. You are spirit beings of another dimension, whom Christ wants to guide home through the Father's love, through the Redemption of the Son, who is the Mercy.

Amen.

Fourth Level of the Soul
(Earnestness)

My peace and My love are with you. Open your hearts for the word of My life. It should penetrate the inner spheres, for I Am the life. The words are not spoken for the human senses, but especially for the heart. If you take in the words with your intellect, you will not have the spiritual aspect, for the Spirit of infinite love is in you! As soon as the person opens himself for the divine Spirit, He will become noticeable in the soul and in the person, for Spirit is movement. If the person affirms the Spirit of God, then He will convey much to the person, including what he has not yet understood in the words that are here.

Open yourselves to the infinite love, which prevails in all hearts and wants to unfold. Your souls should be prepared, because the person, who is in the school of life called "world," should prove himself, so that one day soul and spirit can enter the higher consciousness levels.

What does it look like for the human race? What does it think about God, the eternal Father? What does humankind think about Christ, its Redeemer? Redemption, which took place about 2,000 years ago on the hill of Golgotha, is in each soul. It is the "I Am," the omnipresent Spirit that speaks to you human beings. Your souls should prepare themselves for God. The preparation can take place only when you become conscious children of God, for it is written in the Holy Scriptures: *"Become like the little children, for theirs is the kingdom of heaven."* Where does the person seek his heaven? Outside of his eternal self or in himself? I say to you: Seek heaven in yourselves and become like the little children. Only then, is the inner Kingdom of God near to you, and the soul will find its way to Me, which I have opened for each and every soul.

My dear children, awaken in the soul and hear the voice of your Redeemer, who guides the souls through all the purification levels. Happy the person and the soul who have recognized salvation on this Earth and in this school of life. The high consciousness of the "I Am" should be opened in each soul. It begins with the eternal Order of the Father. Put order in your thoughts; fulfill His Will. Respect His Intelligence and listen to His admonishing voice, the Earnestness, because God, our eternal Father, is the life of the soul. The characteristics, also called natures of God, are the levels of the law of the soul. These consciousness levels are divine heavens as well as purification planes. They have to completely unfold in the soul. This takes place only by way of self-recognition and a corresponding life.

The level of Earnestness is the prevailing Creator-Love. In the eternal homeland, this region of light is particularly developed for the mineral, nature and animal kingdoms, since the spiritual collectives do not react to the Father's love, but particularly to the Creator-Love of Earnestness. Each soul has all the attributes and natures in itself, and this is why it has to go through all the levels, that is, to recognize and live them. Only then, will it attain the next higher consciousness. I also call the consciousness levels the life centers of the soul and of the person. If the soul has gone through Order, Will and Wisdom, then it is largely established in its spiritual workings, which means that it has largely stabilized itself. That is why I also call the natures of God the stabilizers of the soul.

On the basic level of Earnestness, all the sub-levels, in turn, have to be activated, that is, the soul must continue to perfect itself, so as to be attracted by the next higher attribute of Patience – which we call the filiation attribute – for everything is based on spiritual gravitation. The one who activates the light can be attracted by the light. The one who persists in his darkness will remain bound to it, until the Christ of God, who is the Love and Mercy, is recognized and lived. After the resurrection, through a reduced spiritual atomic power, I made my ether body visible again for many people. Much was conveyed to the people but they did not understand the meaning and purpose of My work and of the crucifixion, nor of the resurrection. That is why the masses are bound to their views still today. The spiritual energy cannot unfold in the souls of the human beings, since they do not recognize the purpose of My life on Earth.

The soul is the microcosm in the macrocosm. This is why a total harmony between universe and soul has to be established. If this is not the case, then the soul particles remain without spiritual light. This means that they cannot spiritually illumine themselves, because the soul is inhibited through its earthly way of life, and thus, in part, wrongly polarized. Even if it has completed the first three stabilizers and already bears much light within, nevertheless, it is not yet oriented to further levels.

On the basic level of Earnestness, as well, each soul has to recognize all sub-levels and live what it has recognized. Only then, will the soul blossom and awaken to the next higher consciousness. Just as the Earth has its four seasons, the soul, too, has its four stabilizers or natures. They are linked with the filiation attributes, which are likewise in the soul and must blossom into full maturity.

Consciously or unconsciously, every child bears the Father's love in its soul, as well as the Creator-Love. It is the connection to the mineral, nature and animal kingdoms, for everything is contained in all things. The spiritual atomic power is not outside of creation. Creation needs to become a concept of the whole. This takes place especially in these four divine stabilizers or natures, which are, at the same time, the divine characteristics.

What does Creator-Love mean, which the divine Earnestness especially expresses? It means: God is love and all that He created, was created out of love for all life. This is why nature and the animals love the light. Instinctively, they gravitate toward light and warmth. They live through the power of the light. For them, it is the sensation of love. Therefore, the spiritual genus fields sense the light as the fuel of love. The souls and human beings also long for these spiritual substances, which are absorbed by them unnoticed. They are the light of the Spirit, which is given to all life through the four natures of God. Each soul was made up according to this cosmic principle.

I repeat the development of the soul's makeup starting with the mineral. It is a genus form that changes over to nature after it has fully matured, and then enters the animal kingdom. We call the genus forms elements of development. Briefly spoken, this is the development of every perfect soul.

Earnestness is the Creator-Love. It is the light for the spiritual collectives, in particular. The divine collectives mature by way of the first three natures, also called characteristics. In the fourth nature they reach full maturity. The mineral streams as well as the nature elements and animal souls are brought to full maturity by the divine spectral lights. These phases of development take shape in the sphere of development that has its four heavens, or development levels. They are meant solely for the maturing process of the nature souls, which can be raised to the filiation only after having completed their development as a nature being. The minerals only have rays of development. They mature by way of the divine irradiation. Their course of development is completed in the various forms of the nature and animal kingdoms. I will teach about this soul development in due course. This was merely an impression from the great event of infinity.

In the purification plane of Earnestness, each soul has to open these divine regions of light. The course of development of the soul in the basic level and in the sublevels is as follows: The teaching angel instructs the souls, and points out the divine genus fields, in particular, also called the collectives. On the level of Earnestness, the soul is taught the connection to all life. From the level of Order up to the level of Earnestness, each soul was made aware of the spiritual connection with creation and the holistic structure of the soul, which bears everything in itself. In the other natures, the souls have already learned the connection to the principle of creation, but on the level of Earnestness they have to totally live what they were taught.

Each soul has to establish a relationship to all divine life, which is initiated by the cosmic radiation. The love for the Creator and for creation has to fully blossom in the soul. No soul particle may be impure.

On your Earth, you can use words without a deep meaning or feeling, like, for instance: "I love the animals or nature." How often does the human being say: "What a beautiful and precious stone!" The words very often flow without emotion, but on the level of Earnestness, there is only the sensation and not the word. As a maturing soul, the sight of an animal or of divine nature, as well as of minerals, may very well please you, but as long as it is left at that, your soul particles will not receive any light. They remain inert. Only when you love creation from the lowest form of mineral to the perfect nature soul, will your soul become a perfect structure of light. On your Earth, you can reject the worm, the beetle, the fly or the spider – in the realm of development, you stay just as impeded in your soul as on the Earth in an earthly garment. As a human being, you do not see the shadows of your soul, but as a soul you are shown your garment and your insufficiency.

The same applies in the mineral kingdom as well as the animal kingdom. On your planet Earth, you thoughtlessly exploit the life principles of the minerals, and you hardly pay attention to the animals.

That, O human child, is written in the book of life, which is in you – it is your soul! In the realm of development, it is then leafed through, that is, you then see your burdens in your shadowed soul particles. They form your spiritual garment. Just as the Earth's radiation is the atmosphere, so is your soul's radiation your spiritual garment, which shows the condition of your soul. The one who deliberately kills will expiate. Who created the many parasites? I say to you that they are mutations that emerge through the ineptitude of the human being. Who brought the Earth into the state of infertility? Again, the human being. The life on Earth includes animals that I want to call "nature's cleaners." Their cooperation, which is directed from the cosmos, is prevented by the hand of human beings. Their task was to prepare the soil and the waters for human beings, but My children's unknowingness and their life, which is oriented toward exploitation, have destroyed them for the most part.

On the level of Earnestness, all of this must be recognized, expiated and then, what one has become aware of, must be built up in love. Only when the soul bears the true connection to all life, that is, when the soul particles are cleansed and vibrate completely in the light regions of Order, Will, Wisdom and Earnestness, will the soul have stabilized its garment.

Oh see, My dear children, the one who attains knowledge in the school of Earth and also lives it, will have a shorter time of expiation in the soul-garment. The soul is a child of creation, which, through the spiritual inheritance of God-Father's attributes of Patience, Love and Mercy, was raised to a perfect child. All these attributes are the patrimony of the soul.

Therefore, when I say to you "possess the kingdom," then I mean: Enter your spiritual heritage.

Acquired earthly wisdom does little for the soul. It could be suggestions for the divine Wisdom, if the person is made aware of them. That is why it is about: warmth of heart and soul-wisdom before intellectual knowledge! The soul remains tied to whatever the person has bound himself to on Earth, until it is willing to be taught otherwise.

If you are tied to an opinion or a dogma or to a certain way of life, you will also be tied in the spheres of purification. A person who knows about the inner core of being that is in each soul, will reach the regions of light more quickly when he lives according to the commandment of commandments: "Love your God and Father above all and your neighbor as yourself. Love creation in all its details, for the entirety of the Creator is in you."

Only the person who lives in God and recognizes the details of an infinite creation will draw strength in the earthly garment and largely regenerate his soul in the school of life, "Earth." That should be the goal of My children on Earth.

The one who has completed the basic level of Earnestness and its sub-levels is free of the Earth's radiation. He is a so-called semi-angel, who continues to familiarize himself with the patrimony of the Father-Mother-God: Patience, Love and Mercy. These semi-angels are also teaching angels in the four natures or characteristics of God.

The human being has received the tools for this through My sacrifice on Golgotha. The one who lives in Me, and I consciously in Him, knows about his tools, which he also knows how to use in My name. The one who loves Me, loves My Father in heaven, who does His works through Me. The one who loves Me, loves his neighbor, in whom I have also taken up dwelling. The one who loves Me and My Father becomes a child of the divine Father, who instructs it in all forms of life, and this can already take place here on this Earth.

My peace and My knowledge shall take root in you, so that I can reveal even more to you.

Amen.

Fifth, Sixth and Seventh Levels of the Soul (Patience, Love and Mercy)

The almighty eternal Spirit prevails in every single soul. He is loving, helpful and good. He has opened the Earth for love. Through this, love prevails on this Earth. It turns to every soul, eternally. Absorb this love in your hearts and become aware of My consciousness.

I Am the Christ of God, the crucified and resurrected One, the conveyor of these words, so that the person and his soul recognize the eternally prevailing power, which expresses itself in all Being, at every moment of his eternal life. To gain the eternal homeland, the human being and every soul must be permeated with love. Humankind's shortcomings are egoism, greed, stinginess and envy, which produce no warmth of heart, by which the souls cannot unfold for the attributes of God.

Every soul experiences its maturing process to the eternal "I Am." This ascent takes place solely by way of the seven centers of life, which are also called consciousness levels or attributes and natures of God. The Spirit can explain this ascent only when person and soul are spiritually active, by which they reach the goal. The eternal "I Am" gives strength for the ascent to the one who makes an effort, so that he recognizes himself and makes further progress.

O human being, recognize your world and yourself. Only after your recognition does the life begin that you have to live out in order to mature. When the soul recognizes itself, then maturing begins, the striving and the true life in God. As long as person and soul do not recognize themselves, they merely vegetate in the low consciousness "human being" on Earth and in the purification spheres.

The almighty Spirit sent Me, so that the person turns to Love and Mercy and purifies and refreshes his soul in the school of life "Earth," according to the law of life. Only the eternal Spirit is the living wellspring in each soul. As long as the person and soul do not drink from it, the further divine attributes are closed to the soul. Many of My children are very far from the spiritual principles of life, since the divine voice has become foreign to them. For most of My children, God, the Lord, is a mythical creature that stays hidden somewhere.

Through My life as Jesus and My sacrifice on the cross, Satan has been banned, but in the human "ego" a patrimony from Satan still remains. It is the negative thoughts that appear again through the inbred intellect. I call this patrimony the "satan of the senses." It causes confusion among My children and demands proof. It seeks what is real and actual, and does not seek in the "I Am," in the power that is hidden to My children, but in the temporal, which to it is visible and feasible. The intellect keeps the eternal truths imprisoned in the soul. They can be known and experienced only when the person believes and becomes trusting. The intellect is a danger to the soul because with considerable intellectual knowledge, it can be tied down in a purification plane for a long time.

That is why the law of My Father is: soul-wisdom before intellectual knowledge, warmth of heart before intellect! The one who has no heart for his neighbor is not mature enough to enter the God-consciousness. The four soul-stabilizers can be completed only when the commandment of commandments is totally lived: *"Love your God and Father above all and your neighbor as yourself."* The life forms from the mineral kingdom to the animal kingdom and to perfect nature-souls are also contained in this commandment.

External wealth is often a millstone around the soul's neck. Inner wealth makes person and soul free. It directs them to higher insights that are in the filiation attributes of Patience, Love and Mercy. Therefore, open your hearts and ears for the Spirit, because seven basic levels and their sublevels are being maintained in your souls as spiritual principles. All seven times seven have to be opened by the soul.

Jesus of Nazareth, the Christ of God, spoke and speaks: *"You will reap what you sow."* Your thought is decisive for the development in the eternal life. When a human being goes over this Earth without goal or plan, without self-control and self-criticism, the soul can come to great harm, which often can be remedied only in eons. Once the soul has matured through the development of the four natures and enters the further upbuilding levels of Patience, Love and Mercy, then the soul has developed and unfolded for the most part. It is no longer a soul in the sense of burdening; instead, it is nearing perfection.

We call this upward striving soul, which has entered the three filiation attributes, a semi-angel, because the spirit being is shortly before its perfection.

What are the special features of these three spiritual levels? In these regions of light, the semi-angel is taught the connection to the Father-Mother-Principle. In the basic level of Patience the following is especially relevant: "No one comes to the Father except through Me, Christ." Every soul can complete the four purification planes, regardless of whether it believes in the Son of God, its Redeemer, or not.

Those that go through the levels in the awareness of Christ will not have a difficult time in the filiation attributes. However, those spirit children who have not lived in the awareness of Christ, but have striven for the Spirit of God without Christ, will have a hard time. It will now be revealed to them that without the recognition of the Son of God, who is the Co-Regent in the eternal kingdom, the wholeness in their souls cannot unfold.

In these filiation attributes, the children that were taught differently in the earthly garment separate themselves from the Christian teachings. Here it may again be said: People who had more nobleness of heart than intellectual knowledge are also much easier to direct as awakening spirit beings and can be brought closer to the Son of God more quickly than the persistent adherents of a denomination, for whom dogma ranked above all.

Before the gate to heaven, there are planets on which those children of God live who do not accept Me, the Son. My children call these planets wisdom planets. However, they have nothing to do with the divine plane of Wisdom. These semi-wise ones may very well live in the awareness of God, but not in the acknowledgment of Christ. Many beings from these wisdom planets are among the human beings, either in the spiritual garment or incarnated. They are the representatives of these levels of wisdom. The eastern teachings have adopted much from them. These pearls of wisdom should not be despised, since they strive for the consciousness of God, but not for the Redemption that their soul also needs to be able to enter the wholeness of life.

No soul will attain perfection except through Me. I Am the keeper of the divine gate. No one will enter there except through Me. My children, be assiduous with the commandment of love in the name of the Father and of the Son – This is what I ask of you. Carry the gospel of love and redemption to the children who still live apart from the awareness of Christ, for every soul bears the spark of My Redemption, which should be ignited. The three basic levels of Patience, Love and Mercy contain, in turn, the other characteristics, also called natures. The particle structure of the soul and the cosmic attraction are taught anew.

In the soul particles are spiritual elements that are stimulated by the thought, which is a sensation in the spirit being. The divine elements consist of the spiritual makeup. For the better understanding of My children, we call them "fire, water, earth and air." They are of a spiritual nature and form, in turn, the natures of God. These elements are stimulated to a corresponding activity via the spirit being's sensation.

The teaching angels teach as follows: Everything that you see is based on radiation and on the spiritual law of gravitation.

As soon as you think of a spirit being, for instance, you bring the elements in a soul particle into rotation, by which the addressed particle structure orients itself to sending and receiving.

This connection is made at a speed unimaginable to the human being, because eternity is without time and space. Either the spirit being or the semi-angel can perceive the answer in itself, or it can also make the consciousness level, in which the other being dwells, visible in itself, since – as I mentioned – eternity is timeless and spaceless.

The opening of the consciousness level takes place in that the spirit being, or the semi-angel that is present in the schooling, addresses several spiritual particles, by which the divine elements are brought into a higher spiritual vibration, and the spiritual level opens. In this and similar ways, the radiation and the spiritual gravitation are explained to the spiritual pupil on the basic levels of Patience, Love and Mercy.

If a spirit being wants to go from one planet to another, or from one heavenly plane to another, then the elements are again stimulated by way of the divine sensation. Through this, the spirit being can proceed to the spiritual magnetic ray determined by it and through which it is attracted by the planet or the heavenly plane.

My children, this occurrence cannot be measured by the speed of light or by a thought. It takes place at an unimaginable speed. The entire spiritual power of a perfect soul develops during these spiritual exercises.

The teaching angel also instructs the awakening spirit being about the families of the eternal homeland and about the dualities, as well as the soul and kin relations. If the soul has not yet given any value on experience concerning this, the awakening spirit being, also called semi-angel, has to now recognize the all-encompassing life and familiarize itself with it. The question is asked: "Why did God, our Father, call these three filiation attributes to life?" The answer is: Because we are children of God! The teaching angel is asked more questions: "If we are children of God, are we all created or spiritually procreated, as well? Why is God the Father-Mother-God?" The answers of the teaching angel will be as follows: The first creations went forth from the Father-Mother-God. God, the Lord, created male and female spirit beings. "Why did God, the Lord, create male and female spirit beings?" This question is often answered because many of My children have been interested in these spiritual laws already on Earth or in the spiritual purification planes.

The teaching angel will make a very special effort with those semi-angels that know little or nothing, so that this wonderful community life in God, our Father, is brought home to its brothers and sisters. I, Christ, the teaching master of the New Covenant, also teach this to My children in the school of life, Earth.

In the eternal homeland there are duals. They are spiritual pairs. They stemmed from the seven created characteristics of God. These characteristics of God are the first heavenly sons and daughters that were created from the Father-Mother-Principle. The Father and Mother Principles consist of the divine reciprocal action. God unites everything in Himself: Father and Mother, positive and negative.

More spirit beings were procreated from this Father-Mother-Principle. They form the spiritual union. From the spiritual union emerged, and emerge, the extended kin. We call the direct spirit beings that emerged from a dual pair the spiritual union. Other dual-unions from the spiritual unions we call the kin.

However, all children of God come forth from the origin, namely, from His divine reciprocal action, because the God-Father-Mother-Principle flows eternally in all spirit children. It is the power of the Father, who made His children into the children of God, through Patience, Love and Mercy. Into every nature-soul that is raised to a child of God, the Spirit of Love breathed, and breathes, the breath of His life – the Father-Mother-Breath through His attributes of Patience, Love and Mercy.

In the kingdom of My Father, there is neither courtship nor coveting. Instead, all live according to the principle of purity, which is the giving and receiving principle. Every dual-pair, from which more spirit children come forth, lives in the love for the Father-Mother-God and in the union to and with one another. A spiritual procreation is stimulated through a certain divine spectral light. The semi-angels can be told more about this, because they should link with their soul and kin relations. You, My dear children, were, and will be, told more about this as soon as the soul has attained a certain maturity.

On the Earth there are all levels of knowledge. Therefore, this spiritual truth cannot be conveyed to every soul just yet. It will take place only when the soul has the necessary maturity.

The one who asks will receive, that is, the one who wants to have his dual or a spirit being from the soul and kin relations with him, or wants to get to know it, may orient his cosmic soul to this connection. It is the same process that I have already explained. It is the alignment of the spiritual particle structure with the divine elements, by which the desired connection can be established.

We call spiritual thinking sensation, for the spirit beings have neither cells nor organs. They are built in the divine particle structure. Their mentality is the sensation, which is reflected in the spirit particles.

For many semi-angels, it is a great awakening when they see their next spirit kin. In the dual or in another spirit being from the spiritual union, they recognize their guardian spirit, who taught them either when they left the earthly garment or frequently visited and spoke with them during the process of their soul-maturation. Other semi-angels meet their whole spiritual family only when they have passed through the gate to perfection as fully matured spirit beings. In any case, My children, the joy is indescribably great, for at the latest, in the state of perfection, the spiritual family members or the dual are no longer strangers to the spirit being, because everything that was covered up for the Earth and through the burdens is now fully blossomed again. Every soul has to go this path.

It would be advisable for My human children to acquire this knowledge while in the school on Earth, and to live the levels, so that soon after disembodiment, perfection can be attained. Many of these mature souls, semi-angels or, through the perfection, also called spirit beings, have an unspeakable joy in their hearts. The joy of being in the homeland and possessing everything once more, brings many to reflect. They sense the spiritual woe of their brothers and sisters, which means: We, too, are waiting so much for the brothers and sisters, who have already been in the spheres of purification for many light-eons and who enter a cycle of renewed incarnation again and again. Many of the semi-angels or perfect beings still have rather present in them the axioms of the teaching angels, through which they have matured and attained perfection.

And so, their request often is: "We want to go over to the purification planes as semi-angels or as spirit beings, and teach our brothers and sisters the same things that were lovingly taught to us." The semi-angels are often more successful with the stubborn souls than a teaching angel, because they tell about their own progression into God's eternal paradise, which the souls are facing. They speak about the difficulties they had, and how, with the teaching angel, they went about it in order to mature and reach more levels. Through their own experience, many semi-angels have already shown the way for a great number of souls in all the purification planes. The words from My life on Earth can be applied here: "Bear one another's burdens."

The semi-angels also bring many souls that come from non-Christian denominations to the belief in Christ. However, everything takes place under the aspect of free will.

My dear children, these explanations are from your Redeemer, the Christ of God, spoken through a prophetic person. They are given for your spiritual edification and, above all, for the maturity of your soul. My life is in service of My children, whom I want to lead, over these purification and consciousness planes, to the Father and to those who are waiting for them in the spirit.

My work is the work of leading back.

Christ in the Father, together with the messengers of light, will lead you to perfection over these basic levels and sub-levels, also called purification planes.

I leave My peace in your hearts.
Amen.

P.S.: For better understanding: Angels are pure spirit beings. They do not have wings! In the material world these are merely a symbol for speed and protection.

Recommended Reading ...

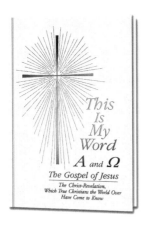

This Is
My Word
A and Ω

The Gospel of Jesus

The Christ-Revelation which true Christians the world over have come to know

This encompassing Christ-Revelation goes way beyond the contents of the Bible. This great work gives an overall picture of what was, of what is – and of what will be.

Building on the "Gospel of Jesus," an existing extra-biblical gospel text, Christ Himself reveals through Gabriele, the prophetess and emissary of God, details of His incarnation in Jesus of Nazareth.

From the contents: Childhood and youth of Jesus – The Falsification of the teaching of Jesus of Nazareth over the past 2000 years – Purpose and meaning of life on Earth – Jesus taught the law of cause and effect – Prerequisites for the healing of the body – Jesus taught about marriage – God does not rage and punish – The teaching of "eternal damnation" is a mockery of God – Jesus exposed scribes and Pharisees as hypocrites – Jesus loved the animals and always spoke up for them – About death, reincarnation and life – The true meaning of the Redeemer Deed of Christ ... and much, much more...

With a short autobiography of Gabriele
1078 pp., softbd, Order No. S007en
ISBN: 978-1-890841-38-6. US$ 15.00

Excerpts available: www.gabriele-publishing-house.com

The Speaking All-Unity

The Word of
the Universal Creator-Spirit

A Cosmic Work of Teaching
and Learning from the School
of Divine Wisdom

Taken from conversations with Gabriele
and compiled by
Martin Kübli and Ulrich Seifert

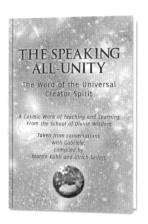

Have you always had the feeling of being connected to a higher power, but not to any religion? Because the teachings were inconsistent, because your questions were not answered or because the religious words and the deeds did not appear to be in accord?

This books will make it possible for you to develop a new image of God. From the Big Bang to the question of why there are addictions, murder and natural disasters, you will find answers to the questions which denominational teachings leave unanswered.

Learn why the respectful and loving treatment of other beings of life is so important, about what we can learn from the animals and how we can live in harmony with nature. And, find out how you, too, can develop a more conscious life: with knowledge, a respectful and loving way of seeing things, meditations, and practice.

Includes an Audio-CD with two meditations:
1. "Everything Is in Bloom" – a meditative virtual walk
2. "Our True Being" – a meditative cosmic view

382 pp., hardbd., many fotos, Order No. S173en
ISBN:978-1-890841-33-1, US$ 29.00

We will be happy
to send you our free catalog

Gabriele Publishing House
P.O. Box 2221,

Deering, NH 03244 – USA

mail@gabriele-publishing-house.com